HARLEY-DAVIDSON
AN AMERICAN CLASSIC

BY DOUG MITCHEL

Publications International, Ltd.

CONTENTS

Louis Weber, C.E.O.
Publications International, Ltd.
7373 North Cicero Avenue
Lincolnwood, Illinois 60646

Permission is never granted for commercial purposes.

Manufactured in USA.

8 7 6 5 4 3 2 1

ISBN: 0-7853-2052-0

PHOTOGRAPHY: All photos in this book by Doug Mitchel.

SPECIAL THANKS: Rev's Vintage Rides, Temple City, CA.; Paul Pfaffle, Vintage Classics, Waukesha, WI; Rex Barret.

OWNERS: Thanks to the owners of the motorcycles featured in this book for their enthusiastic cooperation. They are listed below, along with the page numbers on which their bikes appear:
Dave Kiesow, Illinois Harley-Davidson, Berwyn, IL: 8, 9, 20, 21, 30, 31; Bud Burnett, Bud's Harley-Davidson, Evansville, IN: 10, 11; Tom Baer: 12, 13, 16, 17; Jim Kersting, Kersting's Harley-Davidson, N. Judson, IN: 14, 15, 36, 37, 72,73,78,79; Paul Ross: 22, 23; Henry Hack: 24, 25; Dale Walksler, Wheels Through Time Museum, Mt. Vernon, IL: 28, 29, 32, 33; Henry Hardin Family: 34, 35; Elmer, Kokesh Cycle: 40, 41; Walter E. Cunny: 42, 43; David Monahan, Perfect Timing Inc.: 44, 45; Marvin Bredemeir: 46, 47; John Archacki: 46, 47, 50, 51, 60, 61; Elizabeth Phillips: 52, 53; Don Chasteen: 54, 55; Stewart Ward: 58, 59; Robert Scott: 62, 63; Paul Ross: 66, 67; Al & Pat Doerman: 68, 69; Ted Moran: 70, 71, 76, 77, 88, 89; Rick Bernard: 80, 81; John Kasper: 84, 85; Lake Shore Harley-Davidson, Waukegan, IL: 86, 87; Claudio Rauzi: 90, 91; Heritage Harley-Davidson, Lisle, IL: 92, 93, 94, 95.

Harley-Davidson founders: (from left) William A. Davidson, Walter Davidson, Sr., Arthur Davidson and William S. Harley.

INTRODUCTION

The history of the motorized cycle began back in the late 1800s, yet even before the advent of the internal combustion engine, steam-powered cycles were on the scene. The first "motorcycles" were built in Europe, but the idea quickly spread to the States.

Once the powered bicycle hit U.S. shores, the race was on. No matter where you looked, someone was building their own version of the motorcycle. The formula seemed simple enough: Get a bicycle frame, install an engine, and sell them to the world. There was, however, a bit more to it.

By 1902, the Hendee Manufacturing Company was already building the now-famous Indian motorcycle out on the east coast, utilizing the same basic components that were seen elsewhere. Close on Hendee's heels were three young men who were toiling away in a small wooden building in Wisconsin.

William Harley joined with Arthur and Walter Davidson to construct the first Harley-Davidson motorcycle, which was finally rolled out in 1903. There was really no cutting-edge technology in the design, as they had simply brought together a single-cylinder engine (based on a DeDion design) and a tube-type bicycle frame. Painted in gloss black, that first machine was admired by friends and family—and that's where things started to get interesting.

After viewing the machine in action, several parties expressed an interest in buying one. Until that time, the boys had not given much thought to selling their creation commercially, but the following year, two gleaming motorcycles left their tiny factory. Trimmed by hand with the words "Harley-Davidson Motor Company" on the small fuel tank, they were truly handsome machines. In 1905, they recorded sales of eight motorcycles, and the number jumped to fifty units for 1906.

Seeing this new rage as more than a fad, William A. Davidson, eldest of the three Davidson brothers, joined the

Harley-Davidson's main manufacturing facility in York, Pennsylvania.

fledgling company in 1907. With his help, production rose to nearly 150 cycles that year, and the decision was made to incorporate the business.

William Harley decided to take a break from production to pursue a degree in automotive engineering. The three remaining founders soon had new titles in their own corporation and left their previous occupations to concentrate on building motorcycles. Shortly thereafter, they were working side-by-side with nearly 20 employees in a new brick building.

As the Milwaukee company was growing, so was the interest in motorcycles. Manufacturers were popping up like weeds all across the country, and at the peak, it is estimated that there were nearly 300 different makes. Attrition would soon set in, however, with the numbers dwindling almost as fast as they had grown. But Harley-Davidson would prove to be a survivor—eventually, in fact, the only survivor.

Harley-Davidson had made a name for itself by producing strong, reliable motorcycles and selling them through equally strong and reliable dealerships. While the company enjoyed significant racing success in the late teens, it wasn't speed that sold Harleys as much as reputation. Change came in slow, measured steps; engineering was rarely cutting-edge, but the bikes kept pace with contemporary technology while offering up a healthy serving of style and value.

Harley-Davidson Motor Company, Inc., continues on that same path today. With each passing year, new innovations and improved quality go into each machine that rolls out the door. Of course, like any large-scale manufacturing firm, the company has had its ups and downs. The acquisition by AMF in the late Sixties nearly ended the reign of the proud Harley-Davidson name entirely. But once taken back into the arms of a caring investor group, the chrome once again began to gleam brightly. Today, Harley-Davidson is a household word, and competitors are constantly striving to imitate the company's products. But try as they might, none will ever be able to duplicate the heritage that's an integral part of the Harley mystique.

CHAPTER ONE
THE EARLY YEARS

When William Harley and brothers William and Walter Davidson decided to build their own motorcycle in 1903, the result was rather typical for the period: essentially a bicycle powered by an engine based on a DeDion (of France) design. A large leather belt transferred power to the rear wheel, and starting was accomplished by strenuously pedaling the contraption until the engine sputtered to life.

Since modern mass-production techniques had not yet been instituted, each part of the 10.2-cubic-inch single was handmade. Sporting a vacuum-operated overhead intake valve and mechanical side exhaust valve, the little engine managed to churn out about two horsepower—enough to propel the crude machine at a brisk walking pace.

Though this would hardly seem a marketable mode of transportation, potential customers soon came a-callin'. A second prototype with a larger engine was built later that same year, and it was this machine that formed the basis for the early production versions. A grand total of two "Harley-Davidsons" left the factory the following year, and the boys from Milwaukee were in business.

Production soared to eight units in 1905, when the original factory was doubled in size—to 300 square feet. The next year brought a choice of colors: The traditional black was joined by Renault Gray, both being dressed up with hand-painted stripes. Output rose to 50.

Numerous motorcycle manufacturers were dotting the country by this time, but Harley-Davidson was earning a reputation as a builder of quiet, reliable machines. It was time to take the next step; one that would prove to be monumental for the fledgling company.

Now that motorcycles had proven to be a viable form of transportation, buyers began yearning for more. As one might guess (human nature being as it is), "more" meant greater speed—which in turn meant greater power. Enter the V-twin engine.

Introduced at a motorcycle show late in 1907, the first edition of "the engine that made Milwaukee famous" wasn't an altogether successful design. Still relying on inefficient vacuum intake valves and suffering from belt slip, the original production version introduced in 1909 lasted only a year. Taking a hiatus in 1910, the model returned with mechanically actuated intake-over-exhaust (IOE) valves and a belt tensioning system in 1911, and a legend was born.

With that, Harley-Davidson's technology began advancing at a rapid rate. The company introduced one of the industry's first clutches in 1912, chain drive became available in 1913, and a two-speed rear hub debuted for 1914, followed by a proper three-speed sliding-gear transmission the next year. Singles and V-twins were still offered, and while the former were more popular at first, they would eventually be phased out.

A rather odd fore-and-aft flat twin was introduced in mid-1919 but would last only four years. Meanwhile, the V-twin, which had grown from 50 cubic inches to 61 for 1912, was joined by a 74-cubic-inch version in 1921—the first of the famed "Seventy-fours."

A small-displacement single (21 cid) was introduced in 1926, offered in both side-valve (flathead) and overhead-valve configurations. More successful on the race track than in the showroom, these singles became known as "Peashooters" in reference to their exhaust note.

Strange as it may seem, flathead engines—the crudest of all four-stroke designs—were often considered superior to IOE or even overhead-valve configurations during this period. Though much of the flathead's popularity could be traced to easier servicing (something far more important back then than today), Harley decided it was time to adapt this valve layout to its V-twins, and the famous flatheads—due to survive for more than four decades—would replace the IOE engines as the Roaring Twenties drew to a close.

1910
Model 6

owered by a 30-cubic-inch single cranking out a whopping 4.34 horsepower *(left)*, the 1910 Model 6 brought more riders into the Harley fold. *Bottom, clockwise from top left:* The engine drove the rear wheel via a reinforced leather belt. Though other Harleys were equipped with magnetos, the Model 6 used a battery-excited coil to provide the spark. Leading-link castle forks contained enclosed springs that allowed a small amount of travel; the sprung leather saddle handled suspension duties at the "rear." Carburetion looks crude today, but was far more sophisticated than on earlier models.

Several new features were offered on Harley V-twins for 1915, including a three-speed transmission with tank-mounted shifter *(opposite page, lower left)*, and an automatic oiler that helped prevent under- or over-oiling the 61-cubic-inch V-twin *(lower right)*. Electric lighting was also available, but many riders had more faith in the old acetylene system *(this page, top)*. Suspension systems remained rather primitive, but riders of the day were easily pleased; they were happy to get this sprung leather saddle *(middle)*. Pedals were still included, but floorboards had been added for 1914.

1918 Sport

A rather different approach for Harley-Davidson was the odd Sport model, introduced in mid-1919 to battle Indian's highly successful V-twin Sport Scout. *This page, top and bottom:* Harley's Sport was powered by a 35.6-cubic-inch horizontally opposed fore-and-aft twin driving through a three-speed transmission. *This page, center row, left to right:*

Despite its unconventional engine, the rest was traditional Harley: canister muffler, split (fuel/oil) "fuel" tank in Olive Green, and sprung saddle. The Sport failed to lure many customers away from Indian, and was dropped after 1923.

*G*reat strides were made in styling with the advent of the 1925 line. A new frame placed the saddle three inches lower than before, wider but smaller-diameter tires gave the bike a huskier look, and the fuel tank took on a rounded teardrop shape. *Opposite page, bottom row:* The smooth new tank still held both oil and fuel. A cylindrical tool box was fitted beneath the horn, but many riders complained that it rattled too much and took it off. A more comfortable bucket-style saddle replaced the old flat kind, and could be adjusted to any one of six positions.

Though economical to buy and run, Harley's 21-cubic-inch single never sold very well. Two versions of the engine were offered: a flathead with eight horsepower, and an overhead-valve variant producing twelve horsepower—an impressive 50-percent increase. Both could be fitted with electric lighting, like the flathead model shown. Ordering electric lighting brought a switch panel above the tank *(right)*, along with a generator and battery *(opposite page, top right)*. Because of its lower cost and easier maintenance, the flathead engine *(opposite page, top left)* was more popular than the ohv version.

CHAPTER TWO
THE FLATHEAD IS BORN

Launched in the late summer of 1929, the 45-cubic-inch flat-head V-twin would prove to be Harley's longest-lived power-plant, still being offered in the three-wheeled Servi-Car as late as 1973. In the meantime, it would also see service in the company's military motorcycles that carried American troops during World War II, and be the basis for Harley's racing bikes that tore up dirt tracks during the late Forties and Fifties. Though larger 74- and 80-inch flatheads followed, neither would earn as sterling a reputation for reliability as the good ol' Forty-five.

Seemingly a step backwards in design, the side-valve engine had won many a customer for Indian, Harley's closest competitor. While overhead valve and even F-head (intake over exhaust) configurations were theoretically more efficient, flathead technology had advanced to the point where impressive power output was possible from an engine that remained far easier to service. With the latter being of greater necessity (and therefore of greater importance) in the 1920s than it is today, Indian was gaining ground on what had once been "the world's largest producer of motorcycles."

As it turned out, however, the flathead didn't boost sales the way Harley had hoped—though it wasn't due to any deficiencies in the motorcycle itself. The model's introduction just happened to coincide with the greatest financial disaster the United States had ever known.

Timing plays a big part in the success of any new product, and Harley's timing could not have been much worse. Just a couple of months after the flathead's debut came the infamous stock market crash of October 29, 1929; Black Tuesday. Harley's sales fell from 21,000 in 1929 to less than 4000 during the depths of the Great Depression in 1933.

As the Thirties wore on, however, the economy gradually recovered—as did Harley's sales. Shortly after the Forty-five's introduction came a 74-cid flathead V-twin. Early Seventy-fours had their share of problems, but these were soon sorted out and the machine proved fairly reliable and sold well. A 30.50-cid flathead single debuted about the same time, becoming known as the Thirty-fifty.

As proof of the potency of the new Seventy-four V-twins, horsepower charts from 1929 bore out the fact that the flatheads slightly out-produced similar-sized F-heads, most of the advantage coming (surprisingly) at high rpms. On the road, flathead models had a bit more top end, but acceleration was about the same due to a rather sizable increase in weight.

While V-twins were the focus during this period, Harley continued to build the flathead and overhead-valve 21-cid singles (known as "Peashooters") until the Thirty-fifty flathead single came along for 1930. Though the 21 was brought back for 1932, it lasted only a couple of years. The company also introduced the first of its three-wheeled Servi-Cars in 1932, powered by the 45-cid V-twin. In an effort to further expand the scope of its business during these hard times, other variations were also tried, among them a trio of industrial engines (single, V-twin, and opposed twin), special police motorcycles, and even a special street-painter model designed to lay down the center stripes on streets. And late in 1935, an 80-cubic-inch V-twin was added to the line.

Though the flathead V-twin served the company well during this period, Harley-Davidson felt a more advanced engine would be necessary to keep it competitive in the coming years. Engineers began working on a new overhead-valve V-twin in 1931 that would prove monumental in the company's history after its introduction in 1936.

But even then, the flathead's days were not yet at an end. Harley-Davidson continued to push flathead-powered motorcycles alongside its overhead-valve offerings until the mid-Fifties, and as mentioned earlier, the Servi-Car carried a flathead through 1973. Seems many riders continued to admire the flathead's inherent simplicity, a trait that some associate with Harley-Davidson to this day.

*H*arley-Davidson added some splashy optional graphics for 1931 in an effort to increase sales. The Model D's 45-cubic-inch V-twin came in three versions: low-compression for use with a sidecar (D), standard compression (DL), and high-compression (DLD). Early Forty-fives sported a vertically mounted generator *(right)*. *Opposite page:* The speedometer was driven off of a gearset attached to the rear wheel *(center right)*. Most owners kept the ignition and light switch keys tied together *(lower right)*.

*H*arleys boasted a new tank decal for 1934, which would be used for only two years. The featured bike is painted black with Orlando Orange insets, a no-cost option. Olive Green had been dropped after 1932 as the standard color, being replaced by more vivid two-tones. *This page, top right:* On early Harleys with foot-operated clutches, pushing down with the heel disengaged the clutch, while pushing down with the toe engaged it. *Left:* A small light illuminated the ammeter on the switch panel, and the horn face was embossed with Harley's bar-and-shield logo—an item that today is nearly impossible to find.

1934
VLD

A variety of colorful two-tones were offered for 1934, but this 74-cubic-inch VLD—along with its matching sidecar—is painted in the old Olive hue. *Opposite page:* Styling revisions for 1934 included new streamlined fenders and Airflow taillight (*left center*). *Lower left,* this page and opposite: A small windshield mounted on a protective tonneau shielded the sidecar passenger, and folded forward to ease entry/exit. *Above left:* The chromed rear-facing air intake came along in 1932, adding a touch of class to the bike's profile.

CHAPTER THREE
THE KNUCKLEHEAD HITS

While sales of the flathead V-twins introduced in 1929 had not yet tapered off, Harley-Davidson decided to bring out a more advanced V-twin design for the mid-Thirties. State-of-the-art at that time dictated overhead valves (something Harley already had some experience with from its 21-cid "Peashooters"), so the new engine made use of this feature. Since displacement worked out to 61 cubic inches, the official name for the new V-twin was the 61 OHV. The motorcycle powered by it was called the EL.

Another step forward (at least for Harley-Davidson) was the use of a recirculating lubrication system—a real improvement, as previous models had operated on the "total loss" principal. Total loss systems had a separate tank to store fresh oil, which was gravity fed or pumped through the engine. But what oil didn't get burned off simply leaked out and was deposited on the ground—surely something today's EPA would frown upon. Recirculating systems are the type commonly in use today: Oil is stored in either the bottom of the engine (wet sump) or a separate tank (dry sump), pumped through a filter, circulated around the engine, and returned to the sump to be run through the cycle again—a much cleaner and environmentally friendly setup.

Since the EL carried its oil tank beneath the seat, the tank above the engine now held only fuel. (Previously, the overhead tank was in two parts, one being used to hold oil.) Atop the fuel tank was a new instrument panel that held the speedometer (registering to 100 mph) along with ammeter and oil-pressure gauges. This tank-mounted instrument panel would become a Harley styling trademark that's still in use today.

As introduced in 1936, the EL was an impressive motorcycle, but hardly a flawless one. While other Harleys displaced as much as 80 cubic inches, the new V-twin's more efficient valve layout allowed it to out-perform its larger side-valve stable-mates—as well as most of its domestic competitors. However, oil leaks showed up early, and the frames were found to be too weak to take the added stress of a sidecar. Some of the oiling problems were fixed by midyear, while a stronger frame and further improvements to the lubrication system came for '37.

To riders and collectors alike, these original overhead-valve V-twins have come to be known as Knuckleheads. The nickname refers to the two large bolts that hold each of the right-side rocker covers in place; the bolts look like knuckles on the rocker cover "fists." Incidentally, the very first Knuckleheads had small dome-like covers in place of the bolts; the bolts were instituted as part of the midyear fix for the oil leaks that plagued the early '36 models.

With all the excitement generated by the Knucklehead, it's easy to forget Harley's other models. The 45-, 74-, and 80-cubic-inch flatheads gained styling revisions for 1937 that made them all look similar to the 61 OHV—and each other. They also got a recirculating oiling system that year, and because of all the changes, new factory codes as well: the Forty-fives were called the W series, and the big twins were now the U series. (They were formerly called the R and V series, respectively.)

Joining the 61 OHV for 1941 was a larger 74-cubic-inch version, the motorcycle it powered being called the FL. The arrival of the 74 OHV led to the demise of the 80-inch flathead U series, though the 74-cubic-inch flathead U models continued, and would be offered through 1948.

World War II prompted both a military version of the Forty-five and a special horizontally opposed flathead twin with shaft drive that was designed for desert use. The former was called the WLA, and 80,000 were built and used by U.S. troops. The latter XA model didn't fare as well; only 1000 were built, and none saw action overseas.

Despite the widespread acclaim the Knucklehead received, its life span was brief—at least by Harley-Davidson standards. It lasted only a dozen years on the market, and since World War II occurred during the midst of its reign, production wasn't all that high. But the Knucklehead formed the basis of all the big twins produced since, and today it is among the most revered of classics.

**1936
EL**

28

*O*ften considered the forerunner of today's V-twins, the 1936 E-series was a revolutionary motorcycle in its day. Though displacing only 61 cubic inches, the overhead-valve layout helped it produce more power than its 74- and 80-cubic-inch flathead siblings. *Top left:* Later christened the "Knucklehead" due to its rocker cover design, early '36 OHVs had smooth round "knuckles"; later in the year, these were changed to larger hexagonal nuts. This air horn was used only on the 61 OHV, and only in 1936. *Top right:* Carried over was the Airflow taillight, but most other styling features were new. A smoother teardrop tank carried the redesigned Harley decal. Another new feature was the tank-mounted instrument panel *(left)*, which remains a Harley styling element to this day.

1938
UL

S till a popular solo machine, the UL carried a higher (5.5:1) compression version of the 74-cubic-inch flathead V-twin. Tank and fender striping were altered for 1938, but little else changed. *Right:* Mounted below the headlight, the chromed horn was as much a styling element as a safety device. *Opposite page:* The air inlet *(right center)* was a mirror image of that used on the 61 OHV, which mounted it on the opposite side of the engine. Exhaust exited through this still-popular defuser *(lower right)*.

The 1939 models received more changes than was usual during this period, most of them visual. There was a new two-toned paint scheme, tank-colored instrument panel, chrome fender strips, and redesigned taillight, all evident on the 61 OHV EL model shown here. *Left:* One mechanical change was the repositioning of Neutral to between Second and Third gears on the four-speed transmission's shift pattern; why this was done is unknown, but it was switched back to the conventional pattern (Neutral between First and Second) the following year. "Cats eye" warning lights on the instrument panel were also new for 1939.

1942
WLA

*T*hough rival Indian also supplied motorcycles to the U.S. military, the bulk of the machines used in battle were Harley WLAs. Wearing the requisite Olive Drab paint, these were 45-cubic-inch W-series bikes fitted with special equipment for wartime use. Early versions had the headlight above the horn; sometime in 1942, their positions were reversed. About 80,000 were built, and many were sold as surplus after the war—some for as little as $25. These surplus WLAs were often stripped down and fitted with aftermarket parts, fueling the rapidly developing customizing trend. In an effort to avoid detection during nighttime travel, military vehicles were fitted with "blackout lights" front and rear *(bottom left and right)* that projected only a small sliver of light.

1942
XA

*R*are when new—and even more so today—the XA military bike was intended for desert use and represented a vast departure from normal Harley practice. Not only did the engine boast horizontally opposed cylinders (mimicking BMWs of the day), but the XA also featured a foot-shift/hand clutch arrangement, shaft drive, and "plunger" rear suspension as used on Indians. Only 1000 were built and none were ever pressed into service, their place being taken by the Jeep. Military specifications called for a large oil bath air cleaner, shields to ward off flying sand *(right)*, and longer forks with an added shock absorber *(opposite page, lower left)*. Though the speedometer reads to 120 mph, a plaque ahead of the seat warns riders not to exceed 65 *(opposite page, lower right)*, and includes pertinent maintenance data.

36

CHAPTER FOUR
THE PANHEAD AGE

Even during the years of World War II, Harley-Davidson refused to rest on its laurels. While 45-cubic-inch flathead WLAs were being built in large volume for the military, engineers were kept busy improving the overhead-valve Knucklehead engine. Most of the resulting changes involved the cylinder heads, which were capped by redesigned rocker covers that looked like upside-down roasting pans. As a result, the revised engine became known as the Panhead—and with that, a new era at Harley-Davidson was begun.

While many felt the Knucklehead's life was cut unduly short, the Panhead that replaced it for 1948 offered some valuable improvements. Most notable of these was a switch to hydraulic valve lifters, which automatically took up any slack in the valvetrain and didn't need constant adjustment. As a result, Panheads produced less engine noise and required less maintenance. They also ran a little cooler, because the heads were now made of aluminum.

Just as monumental as the Panhead engine was the introduction the following year of Hydra-Glide front forks. Trading the old leading-link design (which in essence dated back to 1907) for modern hydraulically damped telescopic forks added a cleaner look while doubling front wheel travel. The '49 model was therefore christened the Hydra-Glide—an official Harley-Davidson designation, unlike "Knuckle-head" and "Panhead," which were nicknames coined by riders—and that name was stamped into the upper fork covers through 1959.

The next few years brought only minor revisions, but 1952 saw the introduction of a hand-clutch/foot-shift option for the Big Twins. Like any change from tradition, this modern arrangement took a while to catch hold. But by mid-decade, most riders had made the switch, and though hand-shifts were offered by Harley through 1978, annual demand only rarely topped 200 units.

More big news came in 1953, though it affected the motorcycle market more than the motorcycles themselves: After nearly 50 years as Harley's arch-rival, the Indian Motorcycle Company finally closed its doors. While the tendency would be to credit Indian's demise to superior products from Harley-Davidson, that wouldn't be altogether accurate. Indian had been suffering since before the war, and though competition from Harley surely didn't help matters, neither did the postwar competition from overseas. And it wasn't helping Harley-Davidson either.

After the war, both Indian and Harley-Davidson offered smaller bikes that more closely rivaled their European challengers. Indian's efforts didn't do the company much good, and Harley's had rather mixed results.

Throughout the Fifties and into the Sixties and Seventies as well, Harley supplemented its Big Twin production with smaller offerings. While the W-series eventually evolved into the famed Sportster, less impressive models also peppered the lineup—which to some, diluted Harley's image. These included diminutive road bikes, scooters, and even dirt bikes.

But back to Harley's stock-in-trade, the Big Twins. After celebrating its 50th Anniversary with some specially trimmed 1954 models (why '54 and not '53 is a mystery, especially since the 90th would later be held in 1993, not '94), Harley unleashed another milestone for 1958: the Duo-Glide. At last, the big Harleys could boast of suspension both front and rear, arriving with that innovation only about a decade or two after once-rival Indian. Unlike Indian's plunger-type setup, however, Harley used a conventional swingarm with dual spring/shock combination.

Though minor alterations were made over the next several years, a major advancement wouldn't come until the Panhead's final season. But a major advancement it was: After 60 years of having to pedal or kick their Harleys to life, riders were finally afforded the luxury of electric starting with the 1965 Electra Glide. Though that name would live on for years to come, the Panhead engine would not. It was time for a change; one that some enthusiasts felt was not necessarily for the better.

**1948
FL**

*T*he Panhead engine introduced in 1948 brought aluminum heads for better cooling and hydraulic lifters for less maintenance. Starting in 1947, the shift pattern for the four-speed transmission was reversed, with First being closest to the rider, Fourth farthest away. Otherwise, the FL was little-changed. *Opposite page, clockwise from top left:* This example has been fitted with a nifty chrome oil filter, which wasn't standard. Tank emblems were carried over from 1947. New serrated exhaust pipes would continue into the Seventies. Tombstone taillight also returned from '47. As before, the front fender light served fashion more than function, but was a notable styling feature.

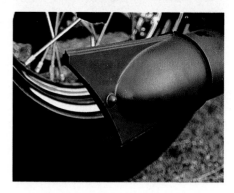

1948
S-125

*T*o appeal to postwar buyers short of funds, Harley-Davidson built the S-125 based on a design by DKW of Germany. Powered by a simple 125-cc two-stroke single driving through a three-speed foot-shift transmission, it sported a girder front fork and rigid frame (no rear suspension). The tank bears the classic "peanut" shape and is nearly identical in appearance to those later used on the Sportster. However, without the tank badge, one would be hard pressed to identify the S-125 as a Harley. The company billed it as an excellent beginner's bike, and records show that more than 10,000 were sold in the first seven months of 1947. Surprisingly, the little bike would survive for 13 years in Harley's lineup with few changes.

S ince the 74- and 80-cubic-inch flatheads were dropped after 1947, the 45-cubic-inch WL was the lone flathead V-twin in Harley's 1948 lineup. It carried most of the same styling cues as the overhead-valve Panheads, so its engine was about the only thing that gave it away. WLs would be succeeded by the flathead K series which ran from 1952–56, and a 45-cubic-inch flathead would continue to power Servi-Cars until 1973.

After releasing the Panhead engine in 1948, Harley surprised its fans with the 1949 introduction of the Hydra-Glide. Named for its modern telescopic forks (replacing the age-old leading-link arrangement), it was the first time a Harley had been given a name rather than just a model designation. Attached to the new front end were handlebars that could be adjusted for position—a novel concept in the Forties. Note the fancy chrome trim on the rear fender (*this column, below*).

1952
FL

The big news for 1952 was the adoption of a modern foot-shift/hand-clutch arrangement for the Big Twins, though traditionalists could still get a hand-shift version—all the way into the Seventies. The Panhead engine again came in two sizes, but not for long; 1952 would see the last of the 61-cubic-inch ELs, as the 74-inch FLs garnered most of the orders. Fuel tanks were enlarged this year, and engines gained chrome-plated piston rings. Fork covers carried the Hydra-Glide logo *(center row, left)*, and would continue through 1959. The color-keyed hand grips and kick pedal were optional accessories, and are very rare today.

1954
FLF

*F*or reasons unknown, Harley-Davidson celebrated its 50th anniversary in 1954, even though the company got its start in 1903—and would later celebrate its 90th anniversary in 1993. Besides boasting a special golden anniversary badge, the '54 models came in a variety of colors, including two-tones where the fenders were in a contrasting color to the tank. A popular dealer option was the addition of color-matched hand grips and kick-start pedal. *Right:* Speedometers now read 1 to 12 rather than 10 to 120, a practice started in 1953. *Opposite page, lower left:* The tank badge remained in script, but lost its underline.

*T*he 45-cubic-inch K series introduced in 1952 had grown to 55 cubic inches by 1954, the resulting KH models providing riders a bit more performance. In either case, a K suffix added to the model name meant the machine was equipped with lower "sport" handlebars, less chrome trim, and more performance-oriented camshafts. But the flathead-powered K was essentially a stop-gap measure until the overhead-valve Sportster was ready, which would happen for 1957; this 1956 KHK, therefore, was the last of the breed, and the last flathead motorcycle Harley would ever offer (save for the three-wheeled Servi-Car). It carries a chromed upper fork cover much like its larger FL brothers *(upper right)*. Unlike the larger FLs, however, it features a modern swing-arm rear suspension with coil-over shocks *(lower right)*.

Since the K-series was getting a lukewarm reception, Harley-Davidson introduced an updated version called the Sportster in 1957—and made an instant hit. With overhead valves topping a 55-cubic-inch V-twin, the Sportster lived up to its name, being far quicker than its predecessor. This example was painted Pepper Red over black; buyers could request the colors be reversed. *Center row, right to left:* Instrument panels held a simple speedometer, while oil pressure and generator warning lights were built into the headlight housing. "Red-eyed" valve-cover bolts were for appearances only. The engine's primary cover left no doubt as to what bike it called home.

1957
FLH

An "H" suffix added to the FL designation denoted a higher-compression engine with hotter cams and polished ports bringing about five more horsepower (advertised as 58-60 versus 53-55). *Top right:* New round tank badges would last only two years—about the norm for this period in Harley's history. Nineteen fifty-seven would mark the end of an era at Harley-Davidson, as it would be the last time the Big Twin would ride on a rigid frame.

*I*ntroduced in 1959 as a performance-oriented on/off-road version of the Sportster, the XLCH was lighter than its XLH sibling, and featured a magneto-generator *(top right)* along with high exhaust pipes, solo seat, smaller "peanut" tank, and semi-knobby tires. It also featured the now-famous "eyebrow" headlight nacelle, still a Sportster trademark. Both versions got a slight horsepower boost through redesigned cams.

1960
FLHF

*H*arley FLs entered the Sixties with a large headlight nacelle similar to that used on the previous year's Sportster. The FLHF designation means this FL boasts the *H*igh-performance engine and *F*oot shift, though the last is not identified on the oil-tank decal *(opposite page, top right)*. Tank badges changed again this year, now featuring an arrowhead theme. Our featured bike wears the popular "2-into-2" crossover exhaust system, which was optional.

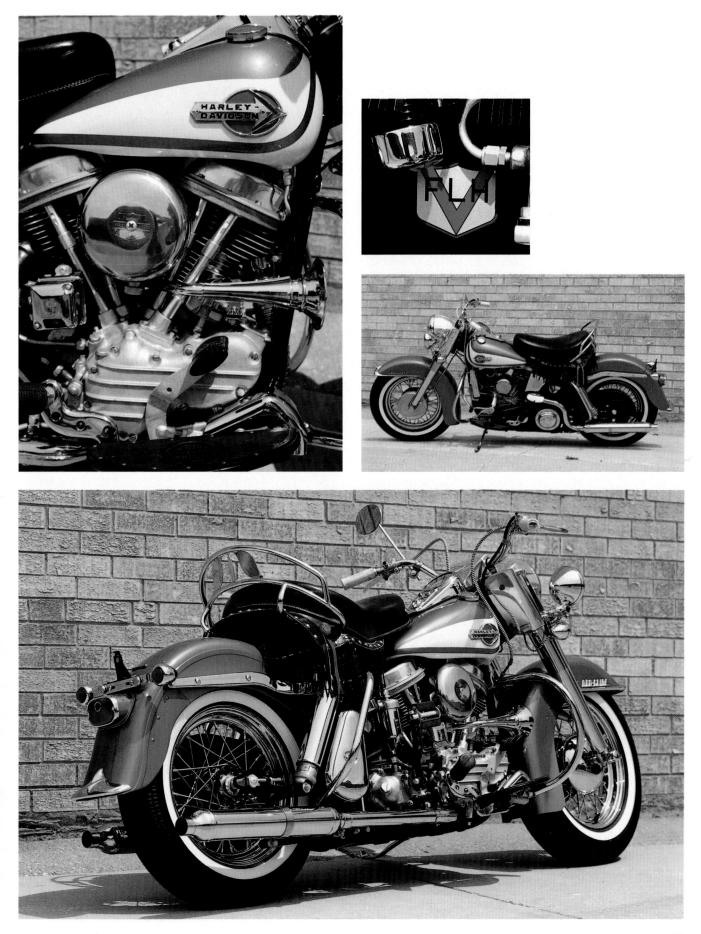

ineteen sixty-five saw the introduction of the electric starter at Harley-Davidson, as well as the last of the venerable Panhead engines. With the addition of an "electric leg," the Duo-Glide became known as the Electra Glide, opening a whole new era for the company. Harley legend was rife with stories of riders being nearly launched over the handlebars while trying to start a recalcitrant engine (some accounts even had riders coming away with broken legs), so the addition of an electric starter on the FLs made them more attractive as touring mounts.

CHAPTER FIVE
THE SHOVELHEAD DIGS IN

The Panhead had just reached its pinnacle in 1965 with the addition of electric starting when Harley-Davidson replaced it with a revised engine boasting (you guessed it) new heads. Called the Shovelhead due to its inverted scoop-shaped valve covers, the engine could now breathe deeper than before, resulting in a 10-percent increase in rated horsepower.

To the casual observer, the new Shovelhead looked much like the Sportster's engine, which was already ten years old by that time. However, the Sportster engine was built in unit with its transmission, whereas the Big Twin, as always, was a separate entity, connected by chain to the transmission behind. And though the Shovelhead has since elicited strong feelings among many riders—some positive, some not—the two decades that the Shovelhead powered Big Twins were perhaps more noteworthy for the changes that occurred in the company than for any changes to the V-twin engine itself.

After going public with its stock in 1965, Harley-Davidson found itself the target of several takeover bids. One of them eventually materialized in the form of a merger with sporting-goods manufacturer American Machine and Foundry (AMF) at the beginning of 1969.

AMF poured money into Harley-Davidson in an effort to expand production, but the conglomerate also stepped in to help dictate policy. This didn't always set well with some long-time Harley managers, and though production did indeed increase, quality tended to go in the opposite direction. It was also during these years that Harley's model line was expanded with a host of small, imported motorcycles—few of which lasted very long and none of which did Harley's image any good.

Of course, hindsight provides a far clearer view than foresight, and the decision to broaden the company's product line by adding smaller, cheaper machines may have been a perfectly logical one at the time. The problem Harley-Davidson faced, however, was the same one that plagued U.S. automakers: The Japanese were far ahead on this score, and it was proving increasingly difficult to beat them at their own game.

Furthermore, Harley's traditional offerings were also being threatened. For a decade after its release, the Sportster was the almost undisputed "King of the drags." By the late Sixties, however, some of the larger British bikes were nipping at its heels, and then Honda really upset the apple cart with its revolutionary 750 Four.

As Harley-Davidson soldiered on through the decade, it became increasingly apparent that hard times lay ahead unless some changes were made. After dumping charges filed against the Japanese manufacturers in April of 1978 proved futile, a handful of Harley executives approached AMF with a plan: In what would later become a rallying cry from owners, dealers, and employees alike, they offered to *buy back* the company.

With profits sluggish and the proposal inviting, AMF agreed to the offer, and in June of 1981, Harley-Davidson was on its own once again. A revived spirit of pride seemed to spread throughout the faithful, and the company's position—and products—slowly improved. The FXR, with its five-speed transmission and isolated drivetrain, added a more modern entry to the line late in 1981, while the next two years brought some interesting Sportster models.

This isn't to say, however, that Harley-Davidson sat on its hands during the AMF years. Indeed, one of the company's most influential products was born under AMF's auspices: the FX Super Glide, the industry's first factory custom.

Introduced in 1971, the Super Glide was not an overwhelming success at first, but it spawned a host of subsequent customs that eventually became Harley's stock in trade. However, perhaps the greatest achievement of the AMF years wouldn't be forthcoming until well after the buy-back program had returned the company to private ownership.

*I*ntroduced in 1961 as a result of a cooperative venture between Harley-Davidson and Aermacchi of Italy, the Sprint boasted a 250-cc horizontal four-stroke single and was quite popular at first. Little had changed by 1966, though styling had become more modern, and by that time, both street and on/off-road (Scrambler) versions were offered. For 1969 the engine was enlarged to 350 ccs on the street-going Sprint—now called the SS—while the Scrambler didn't get the larger engine until 1972. Both models disappeared after 1974, to be replaced by two-stroke machines. *Right center:* Though the crankcase said Harley-Davidson, the engine was built by Aermacchi.

1967
XLH

or 1967, Sportsters gained the electric starter introduced on Big Twins two years earlier—at least the XLH version did. The sportier XLCH kept its kick starter, which remained on the XLH as a backup to the electric leg. As before, the XLH carried fancier trim, including a large polished headlight bezel, chromed rear shock covers, a larger fuel tank, an instrument panel mounted just above the tank *(right)*, and a two-person seat. Despite its luxuries, however, the XLH was outsold by its sportier counterpart in '67.

1968
XLCH

portsters ruled the road in the Sixties, and this '68 XLCH represents the elemental form of the breed. Being a CH (which some felt stood for "Competition Hot") it carries a kick starter and small "peanut" tank, and this example is fitted with a sprung solo saddle. Adding to its sporting appeal are low handlebars and a matte-black covering on top of the fuel tank, which wore the "corporate" badge shared by all Harleys that year.

1971
FX Super
Glide

ustomized motorcycles were all the rage by the early Seventies, but none of the various manufacturers ever offered one off the showroom floor—until Harley brought out the 1971 FX Super Glide. Mating the FL's Big Twin engine and frame with the XL Sportster's lighter front end (complete with "eyebrow" headlight cover) accounted for the FX designation, but it was the fiberglass boat-tail seat/fender combination and buckhorn handlebars that made it a Super Glide. Early Super Glides came only with kick starters; not until 1974 was an electric leg made available. Optional in its debut season was the Sparkling America paint treatment shown on our featured bike, the obvious choice for those patriotic souls who wanted to make a statement while riding the world's first factory custom.

*I*n an attempt to capitalize on the cafe-racing trend that was sweeping the country in the mid-Seventies, Harley-Davidson ventured back into the world of customs to bring out the XLCR. Styled by William "Willie G." Davidson, it applied a small "bikini" fairing, skimpy front fender, angular fuel tank, solo seat with fiberglass tail section, triple disc brakes, and special "siamesed" two-into-two exhaust headers to a standard Sportster, and then cloaked the whole affair in black. Problem was that although the XLCR was claimed to be "the most powerful production cycle Harley-Davidson has ever built," that wasn't saying much; Japanese competitors were quite a bit faster and cheaper to boot. Furthermore, the typical Harley buyer seemed to take little interest in joining the road-racing crowd, so sales never took off, and what was in fact a very interesting motorcycle (and quite soon, a very *collectible* motorcycle) faded away after only two years.

*A*long with the radical XLCR cafe racer came another factory custom for 1977, the FXS Low Rider. More in tune with Harley rider's tastes, the FXS cruiser proved an instant hit, outselling all other models in the line. A matte-black instrument panel perched atop wide "Fat Bob" fuel tanks, while low handlebars and a very low stepped seat combined to give it a dragster look. Both kick and electric starters were provided to bring the 74-cubic-inch Big Twin to life, and nine-spoke cast wheels held triple disc brakes. Originally offered only in metallic gray, black and white were added later in the year. The FXS changed little for 1978, though that would prove to be the final year for the 74-inch version of the Big Twin.

1981 Heritage Edition

*W*ith its skirted fenders, Sixties-style headlight bezel, twin chrome-covered rear shocks, classic Buddy Seat with grab rail, and fringed seat and saddlebags, the 1981 Heritage Edition lived up to its name. Even the rather odd Olive Green and orange paint job struck a chord of years past. The Heritage was one of the first Harley creations to combine the new 80-cubic-inch V-twin—not seen since the Forties—with the retro look; something that is today a standard commodity in Harley's lineup.

1982
FXB
Sturgis

*J*ntroduced in 1982, the FXB was known as the Sturgis, as its first public showing was in Sturgis, South Dakota, during the week-long motorcycle extravaganza held there each summer. The FX nomenclature identifies it as a version of the Low Rider; the B suffix, however, means that it is driven by belts—both primary (engine to transmission) and secondary (transmission to rear wheel)—rather than conventional chains. Completing the factory custom look were extended forks, buckhorn handlebars, stepped king/queen seat, and black paint—acres of it—with just a touch of chrome and orange trim. Popular from the start, the FXB quickly became a modern classic.

CHAPTER SIX
THE EVOLUTION REVOLUTION

Ask ten Shovelhead owners whether they like their bikes, and all will likely give a resoundingly positive response. But ask ten *former* Shovelhead owners whether they liked their bikes, and you'll probably get different reactions altogether. Why the discrepancy? First of all, few people will berate what they currently own. Secondly, most old-time Harley riders are used to vibration and the more-than-occasional breakdown—to them, that's just part of owning a Harley-Davidson. If you've never tasted filet mignon, hamburger will suit you just fine.

When Harley-Davidson introduced the Evolution V2 on some 1984 models, skeptics questioned not so much whether it was an improvement (most felt it had to be), but whether it was improved enough to rival the Japanese V-twins. The cylinders, now aluminum, enclosed the same 80 cubic inches as before, but new heads provided a higher compression ratio while being perfectly contented with regular unleaded gas. Per Harley practice, the valve covers were altered in design, this time displaying smooth, billet-like contours that soon had enthusiasts calling it the Blockhead. Computers were used in the design process, and the end result was an engine that was smoother, quieter, more powerful, and—as time would tell—far more reliable.

Oddly, not every 1984 Big Twin got the Evo engine, and some that did continued with solid engine mounts and a four-speed transmission (isolated mounts and a five-speed had both been offered on some models in the early Eighties). Those that stuck with the Shovelhead all had solid mounts and a four-speed transmission, so there was a wide variety of powertrain choices available.

Those trying to keep the various models straight were faced with an almost impossible task by this time. Sportsters (XL) weren't too hard to keep track of, since minor styling details and equipment levels differentiated most of the bikes. The sole mechanical variation could be found on the exotic XR-1000 introduced in 1983, which carried a dual-carb, aluminum-head engine based on the one used for the XR-750 racer. Big Twins, however, were another story. By now, they could generally be divided into three categories: FL (touring bikes); FX (customs); and FXR (sport/touring).

Within the various categories some acronyms stood out. ST meant Softail, an innovative Harley frame design that looked like the hardtail frames of old, but provided a comforting amount of rear suspension. Introduced along with the Evolution engine in 1984, it has since spread to numerous FL and FX models. STS meant a Softail frame combined with a Springer front fork, which again recalled the look of yesteryear while improving upon its capabilities. WG designated the *Wide Glide*, an FX with widely spaced forks, though those forks were also used on other FX models that didn't carry the *WG* nomenclature. Other than that, there weren't many firm rules.

Making matters worse is that, as indicated previously, not all innovations were found on all bikes at the same time. A five-speed transmission and isolated engine mounts were used on some models of a given year, but not others. Triple disc brakes weren't always universal, and only certain models were blessed with the anti-dive forks introduced on the FXRS of 1983.

The Evolution revolution caught up with the Sportster in 1986, the former 1000-cc engine being replaced by a pair of Evos measuring 883- and 1100-ccs. The latter eventually grew to 1200 ccs, which incidently equates to 74 cubic inches, the same size as the old Big Twin. Sportster choices have expanded of late; for 1996, the tally rests at five.

But the bottom line to all this is that the Evolution models were a greatly improved breed, and today exhibit a level of quality and refinement that wouldn't have been dreamed of by Harley riders of old. Which brings us back to those ten riders who don't miss their Shovelheads.

They're riding Evos.

ot only was the FLSTC a popular choice among Harley enthusiasts, it was also chosen as the subject of a Franklin Mint replica in 1994. With retro styling that dated back to the early Hydra-Glide days, it featured the *de rigueur* softail frame and beefy FL telescopic forks combined with Fifties-style fenders. The seat and saddle bags were dressed with studs and decorative conchos, and fender-tip lights were fitted front and rear.

1988
FXSTS

*W*ith softail rear end and springer front forks, the FXSTS boasted a retro look but with modern mechanicals like front and rear disc brakes, a shock absorber for the front suspension, and belt final drive. Custom touches included a bobbed rear fender, chrome plating for the forks, and Fat Bob tanks with chromed instrument panel. The FXSTS was one of three Harley models chosen to wear special 85th anniversary graphics and badges in 1988.

The last time Harley-Davidson produced a commemorative Sturgis model there had been a Shovelhead engine nestled in the frame; the 1991 FXDB, of course, was powered by the Evolution V-twin—and that engine rested in a new Dynaglide chassis. The special Sturgis model marked the 50th anniversary of the famed Black Hills rally held every summer in Sturgis, South Dakota. As with the first Sturgis built in 1982, the paint scheme centered around black with orange trim—Harley's corporate colors.

C ertainly one of the more outrageous special editions produced by the factory was the 1993 FLSTN, often called the "Cow Glide"—for obvious reasons. Like most of Harley's customs of the period, it carried the Softail frame and belt drive, but differed from the FX specials by utilizing the FL's heavy telescopic forks and retro-look skirted fenders. With its black and white paint and unique bovine trim (even the gas tank and saddle bags carried a hint of heifer), the FLSTN was an instant hit—and an instant sellout. Built only in 1993, just 2,700 copies were produced, insuring the model's status as a future collectible.

*H*arley-Davidson celebrated its 90th anniversary in 1993, and as might be expected, several models came dressed for the occasion with badges and plaques proclaiming their special place in history. One was the FXDWG Wide Glide. Introduced in 1980, the Wide Glide originally got its name from its widely spaced fork tubes, but also came with a 21-inch front wheel, high pull-back handlebars, forward-mounted foot pegs, bobbed rear fender, and a Fat Bob fuel tank sprayed with flames. All those features remained for 1993 except for the last; the Wide Glide came to the anniversary celebration in a two-tone silver tuxedo.

Not all riders like to feel the wind in their face; the FLHTC Ultra was built for those who prefer the luxury of a full-dressed machine. With its plush two-place saddle, electronic cruise control, CB radio, AM/FM cassette player, and cavernous saddlebags and trunk, the Ultra truly lives up to its name. It's the perfect mount for those who like to travel without forfeiting the comforts of home.

INDEX